故園畫憶

庚寅中秋
韓磬江題

《故园画忆系列》编委会

名誉主任：韩启德

主　　任：邵　鸿

委　　员：(按姓氏笔画为序)

万　捷	王秋桂	方李莉	叶培贵
刘魁立	况　晗	严绍璗	吴为山
范贻光	范　芳	孟　白	邵　鸿
岳庆平	郑培凯	唐晓峰	曹兵武

故园画忆系列
MEMORY OF THE OLD HOME IN SKETCHES

黄土高坡的乡土风情
——米脂素记
Local Scenery and Customs of the Loess Plateau

陈化智　绘画　撰文
Sketches & Notes by Chen Huazhi

学苑出版社
Academy Press

图书在版编目（CIP）数据

黄土高坡的乡土风情 / 陈化智绘画、撰文 . —北京：学苑出版社，2017.12

（故园画忆系列）

ISBN 978-7-5077-5418-6

Ⅰ.①黄… Ⅱ.①陈… Ⅲ.①钢笔画—作品集—中国—现代②米脂县—概况 Ⅳ.①J224.8②K924.14

中国版本图书馆CIP数据核字（2018）第016885号

责任编辑：周　鼎
出版发行：学苑出版社
社　　址：北京市丰台区南方庄2号院1号楼
邮政编码：100079
网　　址：www.book001.com
电子信箱：xueyuanpress@163.com
联系电话：010-67601101（营销部）、67603091（总编室）
经　　销：全国新华书店
印　刷　厂：北京赛文印刷有限公司
开本尺寸：889×1194　1/24
印　　张：5.25
字　　数：103千字
图　　幅：103幅
版　　次：2018年3月北京第1版
印　　次：2018年3月北京第1次印刷
定　　价：45.00元

目　录

序　　　　　　　　　　　　李渝基

梁峁塬谷

黄土高原（一）	3
黄土高原（二）	4
黄土梁	5
黄土峁	6
黄土塬	7
黄土峡谷（一）	8
黄土峡谷（二）	9
黄土峡谷（三）	10
黄土峡谷（四）	11
黄土柱	12

窑洞人家

山路（一）	15
山路（二）	16
山路（三）	17
小路	18
山路	19
山路	20
石阶坡道	21
山路	22
坡口	23
土坡	24
窑洞群（一）	25
窑洞群（二）	26
窑洞群（三）	27
窑洞群（四）	28
窑洞群（五）	29
窑洞群（六）	30
坡上人家（一）	31
坡上人家（二）	32
窑洞和院子（一）	33
窑洞和院子（二）	34
窑洞和院子（三）	35
窑洞和院子（四）	36
窑洞和院子（五）	37
窑洞和院子（六）	38
窑洞和院子（七）	39
窑洞和院子（八）	40
窑洞和院子（九）	41
窑洞和院子（十）	42
窑洞和院子（十一）	43

窑洞和院子（十二）	44
窑洞和院子（十三）	45
窑洞和院子（十四）	46
窑洞（一）	47
窑洞（二）	48
窑洞（三）	49
窑洞（四）	50
窑洞（五）	51
窑洞（六）	52
百年老窑洞	53
黄土窑洞	54
窑洞旁的枣林（一）	55
窑洞旁的枣林（二）	56
窑洞旁的枣林（三）	57
窑洞旁的枣林（四）	58
窑门（一）	59
窑门（二）	60
窑门（三）	61
窑门（四）	62
窑门（五）	63
窑门（六）	64
窑门（七）	65
窑门（八）	66
门楼（一）	67
门楼（二）	68
门楼（三）	69
门楼（四）	70

门楼（五）	71
门楼（六）	72
门楼（七）	73
门楼（八）	74
夯土墙	75
巷道	76
羊圈	77
柴草堆（一）	78
柴草堆（二）	79
碾子（一）	80
碾子（二）	81
黄土风情	
耕地（一）	85
耕地（二）	86
耕地（三）	87
耕地（四）	88
移苗	89
捡土豆	90
收秋菜	91
碾"钱钱儿"	92
碾豆子	93
背柴	94
劈柴	95
拉草料（一）	96
拉草料（二）	97
铡草	98

牛车	99	村妇	105
锯木头	100	婆姨	106
打铁	101	孩子（一）	107
看戏	102	孩子（二）	108
社火	103	孩子（三）	109
会歌	104	串门	110

Contents

Preface   Li Yuji

Terrain of the Loess Plateau	
The Loess Plateau (1)	3
The Loess Plateau (2)	4
Loess Ridge	5
Loess Hillock	6
Loess Tableland	7
Loess Canyon (1)	8
Loess Canyon (2)	9
Loess Canyon (3)	10
Loess Canyon (4)	11
Loess Column	12
Cave Dwelling	
Mountain Road (1)	15
Mountain Road (2)	16
Mountain Road (3)	17
Path	18
Mountain Path	19
Mountain Path	20
Stone-step Ramp	21
Mountain Road	22
Hillside	23
Colorful Soil Slope	24
Cave Complexes (1)	25
Cave Complexes (2)	26
Cave Complexes (3)	27
Cave Complexes (4)	28
Cave Complexes (5)	29
Cave Complexes (6)	30
Upper slope family (1)	31
Upper slope family (2)	32
Cave and yard (1)	33
Cave and yard (2)	34
Cave and yard (3)	35
Cave and yard (4)	36
Cave and yard (5)	37
Cave and yard (6)	38
Cave and yard (7)	39
Cave and yard (8)	40
Cave and yard (9)	41
Cave and yard (10)	42
Cave and yard (11)	43
Cave and yard (12)	44
Cave and yard (13)	45

Cave and yard (14)	46	Gatehouse (2)	68
Cave Dwellings (1)	47	Gatehouse (3)	69
Cave Dwellings (2)	48	Gatehouse (4)	70
Cave Dwellings (3)	49	Gatehouse (5)	71
Cave Dwellings (4)	50	Gatehouse (6)	72
Cave Dwellings (5)	51	Gatehouse (7)	73
Cave Dwellings (6)	52	Gatehouse (8)	74
A century-old cave Dwelling	53	Loam Wall	75
Loess Cave Dwelling	54	Laneway	76
Jujube Forest Near Cave Dwellings (1)	55	Sheepfold	77
Jujube Forest Near Cave Dwellings (2)	56	Firewood (1)	78
Jujube Forest Near Cave Dwellings (3)	57	Firewood (2)	79
Jujube Forest Near Cave Dwellings (4)	58	Stone Roller (1)	80
The Gate of Cave (1)	59	Stone Roller (2)	81
The Gate of Cave (2)	60		
The Gate of Cave (3)	61	Customs of the Loess Plateau	
The Gate of Cave (4)	62	Ploughing (1)	85
The Gate of Cave (5)	63	Ploughing (2)	86
The Gate of Cave (6)	64	Ploughing (3)	87
The Gate of Cave (7)	65	Ploughing (4)	88
The Gate of Cave (8)	66	Transplanting	89
Gatehouse (1)	67	Picking potatoes	90

Collecting Autumn Vegetable	91	Blacksmithing	101
Grinding Qianqian	92	Watching Plays	102
Grinding beans	93	Shehuo Carnival	103
Carring Firewood	94	Singing together	104
Chopping Firewood	95	Village Woman	105
Carrying fodder (1)	96	Poyi aunt	106
Carrying fodder (2)	97	Children (1)	107
Chopping Fodder	98	Children (2)	108
Ox Cart	99	Children (3)	109
Sawing Wood	100	Dropping in	110

序

　　陈化智老师是一位执着勤奋的钢笔画家，是中国钢笔画联盟的常务理事。为坚持钢笔画创作，多年来他积极努力，勇于探索与实践，画出了许多优秀的好作品。同时也特别注意去感悟生活，长期以来，四处写生，最钟情的是去陕北描画黄土高坡，追逐那里的乡土风情。他三次赴现场作画，收集、整理出132幅画作，充分显示出他是一位有理想有抱负有追求的新钢笔画家。

　　在他的画作中我们可以看到那些朴实无华的笔触，浸润着对陕北的向往和对黄土地的爱与深情。作为一位负责任的钢笔画艺术家，几十年来，他将自己对硬质线条艺术一往情深的挚爱都在那一张张画上真诚地表达了出来。他肩负着自己心中的使命与责任，用汗水用智慧浇灌着新钢笔画的艺术之花，这一切只因黄土高坡在时时激励着他。

　　2013～2015年，风尘仆仆的画家来到陕北米脂县进行钢笔画写生采风，收集了许多陕北黄土地的资料。每次少则半月，多则一月有余。吃住都在老窑洞，一日三餐与老乡一起吃饭、喝酒聊天，以此了解当地的风土人情和历史，了解老百姓的生活特点。每天他都要去现场速写作画，同时也用镜头记录下山川、大地、窑洞、村民、房舍和当地的历史遗存。画面上的房舍虽破旧但它仍有着一种朴素美，老建筑有着历史底蕴和文化传承。画家用自己严谨、务实、忠诚的创作态度，记录下了陕北米脂的昨天、今天，也使我们看到了它的明天。很高兴看到学苑出版社将陈化智老师这些作品整合出版为《黄土高坡的风土乡情》，这让更多的人看到了黄土高坡的壮丽和黄土地上人民的精神。

艺术可以是人民前进的号角，它可以鼓舞人民的斗志，激励人们的热情，震撼人们的心灵。但愿这些画作，作为一份记忆永远留在我们心中。

李渝基

中国钢笔画联盟主席

2017年9月6日

Preface

Mr. Chen Huazhi is a hard-working sketch artist and the Executive Director of the Chinese Sketch Artist Association. To ensure the excellence of his sketches, he has worked diligently for many years, practicing and daring to explore, and has created many excellent works. At the same time, he also made an effort to fully experience life. For a long time, he has been sketching around the country; however, his favorite place to do so is Northern Shaanxi where he sketches the Loess Plateau and gathers information about local customs. He visited the Loess Plateau three times to sketch and collect subjects. Mr. Chen Huazhi completed 132 drawings during his travels, fully demonstrating that he is an ambitious, innovative sketch artist.

In his drawings, we can see his clear strokes, full of the yearning for Northern Shaanxi and his affection for the "Yellow Earth". As an earnest sketch artist, for decades he has conscientiously expressed his love for this clear-line art form. He assumes the responsibility for this mission in his heart, pursuing sketching with perseverance and innovation. All this comes from the continuous inspiration of the Loess Plateau.

From 2013 to 2015, after exhausting journeys, he came to Mizhi County in Northern Shaanxi to sketch and capture many aspects of the customs in Northern Shaanxi's loess land. Each visit lasted for at least a few weeks to more than a month. Eating all his meals and living in the old cave, and chatting and drinking with local folks, he learned about their customs, history and their outlook on life. Every day, he sketched and took photos of mountains, landscapes, caves, villagers, houses and local historical relics. Although the buildings are old, they still exude a simple charm of local cultural heritage history. With his rigorous, pragmatic and dedicated attitude, he produced a collection of sketches based on the original, charming scenery and the precious architectural style of the Yellow Earth area. "Local Scenery and Customs of the Loess Plateau" created through his passion, depicts past and present Mizhi County in Northern Shaanxi and vividly envisages its future for all to see. We are delighted the Academic Press has gathered Chen's works into the "Local Scenery and Customs of the Loess Plateau", and more people can learn and enjoy the spiritual outlook of the inhabitants and the splendor of the Loess Plateau.

Art can be a clarion call to advance society, lift morale, inspire enthusiasm and refresh the soul. I hope these appealing sketches will last forever.

Li Yuji
Chairman, Chinese Sketch Artist Association
2017-9-6

梁峁塬谷
Terrain of the Loess Plateau

黄土高原（一）

中国的黄土高原的形成，开始于早更新世晚期，相当于120万年前。黄土高原的地貌较复杂，可分为塬、梁、峁三大类型。塬是具有陡峻边缘的桌状平坦地形，梁为条状垄岗，峁是圆形小丘，在米脂这些地貌都能找到。

The Loess Plateau (1)

About 1.2 million years ago, the Loess Plateau in China was formed in late early Pleistocene. The landforms of the Loess Plateau are quite complex, which can be divided into three categories, including tablelands, ridges and hillocks according to their respective shapes.

黄土高原（二）

　　放眼延绵不断的黄土高坡，就像身置巨大的海洋。丘陵的起伏就像是大海的波浪，越是在黎明时分越像。当太阳渐渐升起后，黄土高坡又像一座座金山，金色的山坡上会渐渐出现一层层梯田，一丛丛绿树，一片片窑洞。随着清脆的鸟叫，从山沟里升起淡淡的炊烟，慢慢地在山腰形成一条轻轻的雾，像绕在山腰的一条纱巾。

The Loess Plateau (2)

Seen from afar, the long stretch of Loess Plateau is just like in the midst of vast ocean. The ups and downs of the hills are akin to the waves in the ocean, especially at daybreak. When the sun rises, the Loess Plateau looks like golden hills here and there. Layers of terraced fields, clumps of green trees and blocks of cave dwellings emerge gradually from golden mountain slopes.

黄土梁

  是中国西北黄土高原地区特有的一种地貌形态类型，指平行于沟谷的长条状高地。梁长一般可从上千米至十几千米，梁顶宽可至几十米到几百米，呈鱼脊状往西侧沟谷微倾。陕北地区的黄土梁以宽梁居多。

Loess Ridge

Loess Ridge is a typical kind of landforms of Loess Plateau, on which terraced fields and sloping fields can be cultivated. If you walk in the ravine, the mountains above look huge and precipitous. However, local people still like to walk along the ridges since they are short-cuts between mountains, though seem dangerous.

黄土峁

　　黄土峁是黄土高原的地形之一，坡相对比较陡，而且有浑圆的山丘。峁上有些许树，山腰上有些许窑洞，有的峁上还有大片的坡田和梯田，弯弯的小路，也是黄土高原的特有美景之一。

Loess Hillock

Loess Hillock is one kind of landforms of Loess Plateau, with comparatively steep slopes, and perfectly round massif. There are some trees on the hillocks, some cave dwellings on the hillsides, large pieces of terraced fields and sloping fields on some loess hillocks with curved footpaths, presenting typical scenery of Loess Plateau.

黄土塬

又称黄土平台、黄土桌状高地,它是黄土高原地区的主要农耕区域所在。正因为它的这一功能,黄土高原地区的人民就更加地热爱它。人们在它上面耕种劳作,更是编了优美的山歌来歌颂它。

Loess Tableland

Loess Tablelands, also called as Loess Platforms or Loess Table-shaped Highlands, are the major farming lands in the Loess Platform region. So, it is attributed to the love of the people in the Loess Platform region. People are farming and laboring on the loess tablelands, and eulogizing them with beautiful folk songs.

黄土峡谷（一）

　　黄土峡谷不同于河流峡谷，它是两座山之间形成的峡谷。从峡谷入口顺着峡谷山道往里走，越走越高，而两侧几乎尽是陡峭的山崖，景色非常险峻优美。

Loess Canyon (1)

Loess canyon differentiates from river canyon, which is a canyon between two mountains. The entrance of a canyon always leads along the mountain passes into the depth higher and higher, with cliffy mountains of both sides steeper and steeper. This is really gorgeous scenery.

黄土峡谷（二）

　　峡谷中的地势有些也会比较平坦，这样的地方往往就成了农田，像一片宁静的湖泊。在地无三尺平的黄土高坡，有一块平坦的地非常不易，因此这些平坦的"湖泊"便成了人们粮食的主要产地。

Loess Canyon (2)

Some mountains inside canyon are flat, which are converted into farmlands, appearing like non-liquid lake. A piece of flatland is rarity in the Loess Plateau where flatland barely exists. Walking along the mountain pass into the depth of the canyon, you can see the cliffy mountains higher and higher at both sides.

黄土峡谷（三）

这种侵蚀地貌遇有恶劣的天气，下大雨或过分的干燥，也有崩塌和滑坡的可能，所以人们纷纷避开，但是画画儿的还有搞摄影的人们，比较喜欢这种美丽的景致。

Loess Canyon (3)

This kind of erosional landform is likely to collapse and slide in case of harsh climate such as heavy rain and excessive desiccation. Due to this, people tend to keep away from there, but the painters and photographers are fond of this kind beautiful place.

黄土峡谷（四）

　　高原上由自然崩塌或雨水侵蚀而滑坡的地貌，虽无法用来耕作，但看风景还是很不错的，艺术家们往往从此获得灵感，进行艺术创作。

Loess Canyon (4)
The landform, which has been collapsed naturally or eroded by rain water in the Loess Plateau, cannot be used for cultivation, but is very nice scenery offering inspiration to the artists for creation.

| 黄土柱 |

　　黄土柱并不多见，主要是分布在沟边的柱状黄土体，它是流水沿黄土垂直节理潜蚀和黄土崩塌共同作用下形成的，是黄土陡坡经崩塌残留的黄土部分。黄土柱可高达数米，图中黄土柱并没有完全成型。

Loess Column

Loess Column is rarely found in the groove edges appearing column-shaped loess masses, which was formed by the subsurface erosion and slide by rain water flowing through the vertical fissures of loess. Loess column, several meters high, is the residue part after collapse of the loess steep slopes.

窑洞人家
Cave Dwelling

山路（一）

在黄土高坡上有通往外地的高速公路，有乡间公路，也有村村通的柏油路，而更值得一提的是乡民们自己走出来的路。因上下坡落差出现的弯完全是由山势和坡度决定的,弯弯曲曲的山路形成独特的风景。

Mountain Road (1)

There are expressways linking with other places, country roads, and asphalt roads connecting villages in the Loess Plateau. More remarkable still is the ways stepped out by the local people. There exist road curves due to the mountain terrain and slopes. The winding mountain roads present picturesque scenery.

山路（二）

黄土高原上到处都是土路、山路。走在山道上才能看见黄土高原的连绵起伏，走山道才能攀上黄土高坡的山顶，看见黄土高原的雄浑大气。山道在黄土高坡上纵横交错像一张网，曲曲折折像一条条有弹力的线。

Mountain Road (2)

There are all kinds of earth and mountain roads in the Loess Plateau far and near. It is on the mountain roads that the continuous rise and fall of the Loess Plateau can be seen, the peak of the Loess Plateau can be reached viewing the vastness magnificence of the Loess Plateau. The mountain roads in the Loess Plateau present an intertwining net and curved lines.

> 山路（三）

　　这是一条上山的主道，比较宽的黄土路，用于运送农具和粮食、水果等。

Mountain Road (3)

This is a main road towards mountains, a comparatively wide loess road, used for transporting farm tools, grain and fruits etc.

小 路

　　这是小道中最省力的，在山梁上的路可以直接省去绕路，多为爬山时从这山到那山的捷径。而人们经过这曲曲折折的山路后，也就看见了近在咫尺的家。

Path

This kind of path is quite laborsaving. Walking on the mountain ridges can save you taking a roundabout way, so it is a short-cut when you climb mountains from here to there. It is easy for the local people to reach home through this kind of winding paths.

〔 山 路 〕

  上山的小路多为窑洞之间联系的路，多就势而行。人们经常走自然走出了路，有的路很窄，仅一人才能通过，也是这地方最多的路。这种小路多崎岖狭窄，如果多人行走则容易发生危险。

Mountain Path

This kind of path is the connecting way among cave dwellings, naturally formed by local people stepping routinely. Most of this kind of path is quite narrow barely for one person through. Many down paths are precipitous; it might be dangerous if several people walk along together.

山 路

　　房屋、窑洞之间的小路便于邻居串门聊天，来往交流，由于人们经常走，又称为鞋子磨出来的路。人们来来往往，经过这一条条熟悉的小路，感情更深厚了，村落间的联系更多了。即使是夜晚独自行走，也不觉得孤单。

Mountain Path

This kind of path, connecting houses and cave dwellings, offers convenience for the local people to drop around and socialize with each other. It is also called "path stepped by shoes" since people always walk along it. Frequent dropping around on this kind of familiar paths enhances the friendship with each other, promoting the communication among villages. People will not feel lonely even walking alone on it at deep night.

石阶坡道

　　石阶坡道是用片状石头竖起并排砌筑的石头路，只能行人步行，大多数都是在高高的陡坡上人家门前的一小段。

Stone-step Ramp

Stone-step ramp is a pedestrian way laid with pieces of stone vertically. Most of them exist in the front part outside of a house building on the steep gradient.

山 路

为了解决黄土高坡上村民的出行问题，而修建的柏油路，每天都有多班班车往来于各村之间。路两旁既可以看到山峦起伏的黄土高坡，也有千姿百态的窑洞，是黄土高原的另一番风景。第一次来这里的人们会惊讶地发现，柏油路联通了村内与村外两个世界。

Mountain Road

Asphalt roads help villagers go outside, and there are several buses commuting among the villages. Along both sides of the asphalts roads, you can see rolling loess plateau, all sorts of cave dwellings, which presents special landscape of the loess plateau. The newcomers will be surprised that it is asphalt roads that connect the villages and outside world.

坡 口

　　黄土高坡中间一条下山的小道，一面长着茂密的红柳和一棵棵小枣树，另一面是陡坡上一片片杂草。顺着发暗的坡口看下去，是两排很整齐的石砌窑洞，中间一条小道。小道两侧就是窑洞的院子了。从高处看，窑洞的院子整齐有序，象城市里的排房。这在黄土高坡上也是少有的。

Hillside

There is a trail in the middle of the Loess Plateau down the mountain, thick red willows and jujube trees grow on one side, and on the other side are patches of weeds on the steep slopes. Seen from hillside, the dark slope are two rows of neat stone caves with a path between them. On either side of the path are the court yards of the cave dwellings.

土 坡

秋天的黄土高原，色彩是很丰富的。进入收获的季节，山上颜色红一块，绿一块，黄一块，美不胜收。加上窑洞的灰白色，整个景色鲜亮而且厚重。这个季节的主色调是金黄色，与主色调产生对比的色调呈紫色和红色。个别的树叶在阳光下，显出春天才有的浅绿偏黄的斑块。

Colorful Soil Slope

The Loess Plateau in autumn, turns into a colorful scenery. In harvest season, the mountains are dyed with patches of red, green and yellow, which is a feast for the eyes. With the gray of cave dwellings, golden yellow is the dominant hue of this season, contrasting with the color of purple and red. Some leaves show light green yellow patches in the sunlight, which usually is presented in spring.

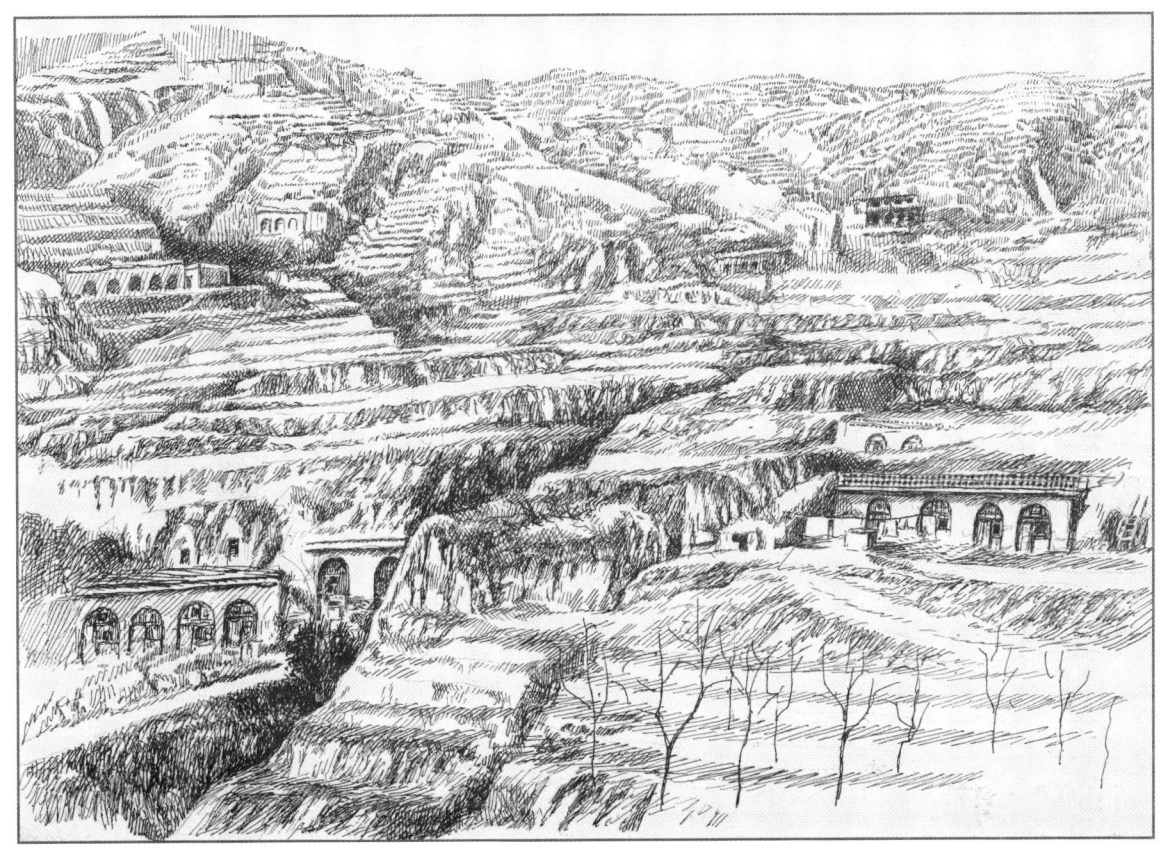

窑洞群（一）

一座座青山紧相连，一层层梯田一层层绿，一条条小路绕山间，这不仅是歌中唱的风景，也是米脂一带黄土高坡的现实面貌。像这样美丽的高土高原景色随处可见。

Cave Complexes (1)

Castle Peaks are closely linked with one another, layers of green terraced fields, paths encircle the mountains, which are not just the scenery in a song, but the reality of Loess Plateau in Mizhi County. Such a beautiful view can be seen everywhere in the Loess Plateau.

窑洞群（二）

在黄土丘陵有着许多这样的窑洞群，窑洞之间有小道相连，也有较宽的村道通向山外。在窑洞附近分布着大小不等的梯田和坡田，还有些果树在窑洞附近生长，也是这里最常见的窑洞布局形式。

Cave Complexes (2)

There are many cave complexes on the Loess hill, among which are the linking paths and wider village roads connected with the outside. Terraced fields and sloping fields of unequal sizes are distributed near the cave dwellings with some fruits trees nearby, which is also the most common layout form of cave dwellings here.

窑洞群（三）

　　黄土高坡所以美丽不仅是山川的美丽，一个重要的元素是有各具情态的窑洞。这些窑洞虽没有统一规划，却能与周围地形，树木巧妙结合，浑为一体。大部分窑洞依山而建，没有华丽的装饰，但朴素大方。依各自生活的需要还设有窑洞式的晾房、仓库、牲畜窑及储备果品、食物的窑洞，都依各自使用的方便合理布局。

Cave Complexes (3)

The beauty of Loess Plateau, not only owes to its mountains and rivers, but also to the cave dwellings with various modalities. These caves are perfectly integrated with the surrounding terrain and trees with no any unified planning. Most of the cave dwellings are built on the hillside, without any decoration, but plain and dignified.

窑洞群（四）

　　村中居住的窑洞多朝阳，很少面对西北，这样也是避开冬季西北风的缘故。有许多的窑洞院落整齐、干净、井井有条，有的院旁还有果树，有的还开辟了菜地。近几年，窑洞还通了互联网，安装了太阳能灶、太阳能热水器、卫星电视。修起了给排水设施，设置了独立的卫生间、厨房。极大地提高了生活质量和水平，正朝着现代干净、环保、绿色、美丽的目标前进。

Cave Complexes (4)

Most of the cave dwellings in the village face the south, rarely facing the northwest to avoid cold wind in winter. Many cave dwelling courtyards are neat and clean and the inner space is in good order. Some of the courtyard have fruit trees, and some also have reclaimed vegetable gardens. In recent years, cave dwellings have also been connected to the Internet, equipped with solar ovens, solar water heaters, satellite TV, photovoltaic power generator, water supply and drainage facilities, independent bathroom, kitchen, and washing room.

窑洞群（五）

随着时代的变迁，不知从什么时候起，住在窑洞的人想离开窑洞领略一下外面的世界。而久居城市的人象发现新大陆一样愿意体验一下窑洞生活的美好。这两种体验都无可厚非。在黄土高坡上的窑洞生活了世世代代的中华儿女，无论你走到哪里也不能忘记这里积淀着中华民族淳朴善良，勤劳智慧的文化。

Cave Complexes (5)

With the change of times, since sometime, people living in cave dwellings have yearned to leave the cave to have a taste of the outside world. And those who live in the city are willing to experience the beauty of cave life, like the discovery of a new continent. On the Loess Plateau, cave dwellings accommodate generations of the offspring of the Yellow Emperor, so no matter where you go, you cannot forget this place featuring Chinese culture which is simple, kind-hearted, hard-working and intelligent.

窑洞群（六）

  大部分窑洞依山而建，没有华丽的装饰，但朴素大方。依各自生活的需要还设有窑洞式的晾房、仓库、牲畜窑及储备果品、食物的窑洞，都依各自使用的方便合理布局。

Cave Complexes (6)

Most of the caves are built on the hillside without ornate decoration, but plain and dignified. In accordance with the needs of their own lives, there are cave-type drying rooms, warehouses, livestock kilns and caves for storage of fruit and food, with reasonable layout for their own convenience.

坡上人家（一）

这是村子边的侧面，能看到山村沿坡而建的状况。这里窑洞不少是一半在山上挖的，一半是用石头砌筑的。明显感到这家的院子已是下一家的房顶。村道的边、沿也用石头砌筑，以防雨水冲刷而塌陷，路面也砌了些石头用来防滑。

Upper slope family (1)

This is the east flank of the mountain village, from where you can see the mountain village built along the slope. Quite a few cave dwellings here are half dug in mountain and half built with stone. The edge of the village road is built by stones to protect against rain and collapse, and the pavement is also made of stone, not very flat but antiskid.

坡上人家（二）

陡坡上的窑洞，长满杂草的山坡中间有一条小道，人们顺着小道上山或下山。一切都是那样的平静。时不时会听到此起彼伏的鸟叫声，这就是坡上人家的印象。置身这样的环境你会忘掉城市里的喧哗和烦扰，新鲜的空气，宁静的村庄，纯朴的民风，会让来到此处的都市人真正体会到放松和惬意。

Upper slope family (2)

Besides a cave on steep slope, along a path in the middle of a weedy hillside, people follow the path up or down the mountain occasionally. Everything is so quiet. At this time, it can be quite common to hear birds calling one after another. This is the impression of the upper slope family. In such an environment, you will forget the noise and annoyance of the city, because of the fresh air, little pollution, simple folk, so staying here for a few days is a kind of enjoyment if time permitting.

窑洞和院子（一）

现在许多窑洞院落除了在使用新型的建筑材料外，在样式和装饰效果上也比以前讲究了，有的住户开始在门前设计垃圾桶。村里有人专门从事清理户外垃圾的工作。村里也用上了自来水，村民的生活方便多了。

Cave and yard (1)

Now, many cave dwelling courtyards are built with new construction materials. Besides, they are more elaborate in style and decoration than previous, and some householders begin to design trash cans in front of doors. Some people in the village are responsible for cleaning outdoor garbage. The village also use tap water, making the village life more convenient.

窑洞和院子（二）

　　这里村民大多家里都饲养有小狗、小鸡、小猫等。一旦有生人来，老远就听到狗叫声，这里的狗都是小型普通狗，没有对人的攻击能力，而且都拴有狗链，仅向主人通报有人来了，好比城市住家的门铃。

Cave and yard (2)

Most of the villagers have poultry or puppies, chickens, kittens at home, but no pig. Once strangers come, you can hear the barking of dog from afar. The dogs here are small, common dogs, unaggressive to people, and they are chained, so they merely serve as doorbell when someone is coming.

窑洞和院子（三）

在黄土高原窑洞前宽敞的院子里种着自己想吃的各种蔬菜，不用去买，不施化肥和农药，随时吃随时可摘，是真正无污染的新鲜蔬菜，这是城里人羡慕的生活。

Cave and yard (3)

All kinds of wanted vegetables are planted in spacious front yards, saving the journey to market. Free of chemical fertilizers, pesticides or pollution, the fresh vegetables can be picked at any time, which is the envy of city dwellers. Plenty of these gardens lie in front of the cave dwellings.

窑洞和院子（四）

这里蔬菜种植仍然保留着自给自足的方式，根据自家的喜好栽种，品种有白菜、西红柿、豆角、萝卜、茄子等。这两颗自家院里的白菜，在秋天仍留在地里，我看只有一个理由就是为了保鲜，随吃随取。

Cave and yard (4)

Here, vegetable planting remains in a self-sufficient way. According to preference, varieties of cabbage, tomatoes, beans, radishes, eggplant, etc. are planted, besides sweet potatoes and peanuts. Two Chinese cabbages in the yard remain in the ground in autumn, and the reason of this is to keep them fresh.

窑洞和院子（五）

这是一处院落宽大的人家，院子前面是陡峭的山崖，院子建在崖上，但院落的主人把院子修缮得非常平坦且能接受充足的阳光。这是一排五孔的窑洞住户，这种既有窑洞又有院子当初建设可想是付出了巨大的劳动和心血。

Cave and yard (5)

It is a large courtyard, with a steep cliff in front, because the yard is on the cliffs, but the owner of the yard makes the yard very flat for enough sunlight. This is a courtyard with a row of five cave households, featuring spatial yards and caves. It is believed that they were built upon a great labor and painstaking effort.

窑洞和院子（六）

　　太阳刚刚升起，山坡下的窑洞院子里炊烟袅袅，户主正在整理晾晒新出的红枣，阳光轻轻的洒在院子里，既详和又温暖。

Cave and yard (6)

With the sun just on the horizon, seen from the side of the hill, a family are cooking, while clearing and drying harvested red dates, a plume of smoke showing the sense of life.

窑洞和院子（七）

窑洞依山而建，而窑洞前的院子居然还有院套院的。这种院套院是你进了一家院后你会发现院里还有一个院门，打开以后便进了另一个有着几孔窑的院子，甚至还有一个并不被人发现的便道可以上山或下山。这两个院无论你从哪个方向来都可以从院子里穿过，这院中院为主人的宅院增加了几分神秘感，也许是更方便的一种形式。

Cave and yard (7)

The caves are built on hillside, but unexpectedly, some court yards before the cave are inside another yard, which means, when you enter a yard, you will find there is a gate leading to another yard with a few caves, and even there is a hidden shortcut by which you can go up or down the mountain.

窑洞和院子（八）

　　深秋，上午九点钟的太阳从东山坡上升起，阳光照在西面较突出的坡上，一片金光，与周围没有被照到的地方形成鲜明的对比，奏出了一组光与影的欢歌，似乎这些窑洞正在享受太阳的光顾。

Cave and yard (8)

Late autumn, nine o'clock in the morning, when the sun rises from the east slope, and shines on the prominent slopes with golden light, which makes sharp contrast to the places in shade. Refreshing and cheering, the sun light seemingly favors these caves.

窑洞和院子（九）

依坡建窑不容易，门前再修个平坦的小院就更不容易了。一是受到地形的限制修起一个平整的小院必须用土填平这一段坡。填土之前要先在下面修起一个挡土墙,然后填埋的土才能形成一块平地。二是动用大型挖掘机械或人工将斜的山坡铲出一个坡道通往上下山，挖出一个垂直剖面再挖窑洞，然后利用余土修出一块平面的院子。黄土坡上的美丽窑洞小院是勤劳和智慧的结晶。

Cave and yard (9)

The small courtyard on the slope is manmade. It is not easy to build a cave against slopes, and it's even harder to build a flat yard in front of gate. First, restricted by the terrain, a courtyard need much earth to level up the slope. Second, large mining machines or manual work is need to shovel a sloping hillside to go up and down the mountain, and dig a vertical section to build the cave. Then, a flat courtyard is built out of the remaining earth. The beautiful cave house on the Loess slope is the crystallization of diligence and wisdom.

窑洞和院子（十）

窑洞是石头砌筑的，门楼是石头砌筑的，围墙是石头砌筑的，院内地面入院的道路和上山的坡道都是用石头采取防滑方式砌筑的。这些用石头砌筑出来的空间，坚固耐用，历经时间的沧桑依然屹立在黄土高坡之上。

Cave and yard (10)

The cave is made of stone, so is the gatehouse. The road in the courtyard and the slope of the hill are both paved with stone in an antiskid way. Although it seems to be a bit weathered, but still inhabited and very firm.

窑洞和院子（十一）

这是一个两层窑洞的院子。上面一层用修窑洞的土垫出院子，边上用石头砌筑挡土墙并修出上下用的梯道。这也许是这里最早的窑洞楼房。陡坡上的窑洞明显利用了地势的特征,而各家格局形式又都不一样。虽然相互靠近，但各是各的院落，看起来院子还有高有低，式样各异，美不胜收。

Cave and yard (11)

This is a two-story cave. For the upper floor, the courtyard is built out of the earth dug from the cave. The stairway and the wall against its sides are paved with stone. Here is probably the oldest cave dwelling. The caves on the steep slope obviously take advantage of the terrain, so the layouts are different.

窑洞和院子（十二）

　　院中的几棵老树显示出这是一个居住很久的院落。高高的玉米垛，隐约地牛棚，丰富的柴草，说明这户人家的收获颇丰。院内的物件非常自然，没有人为的摆设感，是一个老窑洞院子的真实体现。

Cave and yard (12)
A few old trees in the courtyard make people know its long time of habitation. The high corn crib, looming bullpen, abundant firewood, show the family's harvest. The objects in the yard are very natural, without artificial decoration, which is a true reflection of the old cave yard.

窑洞和院子（十三）

　　这座库房的窑洞显然是放不了过多的玉米，在院子里架起了玉米垛，旁边堆砌的石料预示着将来还得再建一座新窑，老旧的磨盘石已经成为卫星电视天线的底座。这个院显得有些拥挤。

Cave and yard (13)

Obviously, this cave which is used as a warehouse, cannot contain too much harvested corn, so a corn pile is set up in the yard. The stones stacked beside indicate a new cave will be built in the future. The old millstone has served as the base for the satellite TV antenna. The yard seems a bit crowded.

窑洞和院子（十四）

在枣树环绕的窑洞院子里，已经褪去的最后一抹阳光，说明天色将晚了。一家人坐在饭桌前似乎在等待劳动归来的人，此时外面传来脚步声，耳朵尖的小女儿拉着妈妈的手嚷道，"我爸回来了"。这是一个和谐的农家院，一个温馨的农家。

Cave and yard (14)

In the cave courtyard surrounded by jujube trees, the last fading sunlight indicates that the night is coming. The family sitting at the table seem to be waiting for someone who will come back from the farm. When footsteps come from outside, the little girl with keen ears takes her mother's hand and shouts, "Daddy is back."

窑洞（一）

　　石砌窑是指里外一致的石砌窑洞，从外面看石料的砌筑没有粉饰更显沧桑，但石头的自然紧密对缝更显出建筑工艺的精湛，如今已很少用来住人，或闲置，或做仓库。

Cave Dwellings (1)

Stone cave refers to the cave that is built both inside and outside with stone. Seen from the outside, stone masonry is more of vicissitudes without whitewash, but the natural closeness of stone shows the exquisite workmanship of the construction. Stone caves are now rarely used to live in, but are used as warehouses or lie idle.

窑洞（二）

黄土高坡上有在一排建多个窑洞习惯，可供家族人员全部住在一个院里，也有窑洞建一排，而院子好几个，可能是分家居住各自保持一种安静吧。常见两座或三座窑洞连在一起的，也有一连五座或更多的连接窑洞。

Cave Dwellings (2)

On the Loess hill, several cave dwellings are normally built in a row, allowing for all family members living in a courtyard. There are also caves built in a row with several yards. Maybe families live separately so as to have less disturbance. Commonly two or three cave houses are linked together, sometimes five or more.

窑洞（三）

近些年，外出打工和移出本地人口增加，导致不少窑洞被荒废，同时被荒废的还有一些陈旧的农业生产工具，每每看到这些总有一些伤感。无论怎样，窑洞毕竟是黄土高坡上人们的主要居住形式，也是需要传承的。

Cave Dwellings (3)

In recent years, more people work out and move out so many cave dwellings have been abandoned along with some obsolete agricultural tools, which always makes people sad. No matter what, after all, the cave dwelling is the main habitat building for people in the Loess Plateau, and it also needs inheriting.

> 窑洞（四）

　　这些闲置的窑洞，可能被它的主人渐渐忘记。但作为一个历史遗存，作为美术采风和创作它又是重要的素材和可参考的资料。

Cave Dwellings (4)

These idle caves may be gradually forgotten by their owners. But as historical relics, they are also important reference materials for the art creation.

窑洞（五）

　　这是个百年老窑洞建筑，现废弃。此窑形状有点像碉楼，门洞里有石台阶样的梯道直通窑顶，而窑顶没有封顶，楼梯两侧还有扶手。这是上下两层的窑洞院落通道，属下面一层通往上面一层的楼梯通道，而上面一层如今已不复存在。

Cave Dwellings (5)

This is a 100-year-old cave building, but has now been abandoned. The cave is shaped like towers, and inside the doorway is ladder-like stone steps straight up to the cave crown, while the crown has not been completed, with stairs and handrails on both sides. The courtyard passageway connects two layers, serving as the stair between the lower floor and the upper one, and the upper one no longer exists.

窑洞（六）

坡道上的窑洞是依山而建的，尤其是石砌窑洞，坚固气派，给人井然有序步步登高的感觉。这座窑洞始建于明末清初，至今仍坚固整齐，是值得作为文化遗址保留的，是中国窑洞中的精品。

Cave Dwellings (6)

The cave on the ramp is also built along the hill, especially the stone cave, showing an order layout when people go up step by step. This cave was built in the late Ming and the early Qing Dynasty (A.D.1600-1700). So far, it is still strong and tidy, worth preserving as a cultural site. It is the best Chinese cave dwelling.

百年老窑洞

全石料砌筑,用工严谨,依山而建。并修了上山的石阶,经百年仍然坚固。窑洞分上中下三层,最高处现仍住人,中间一层保持完好但已不住人了,最下面一层是作为养殖牲畜和仓库用的,现已闲置。像这样的窑洞还有几处,有的窑洞住户已记不清楚建筑年代,有的几易主人,无法考证。所值得称道的是,建窑洞使用的大量石料皆取自当地山下,多为片石,精选石料形状,大小互相吻合,对缝严密。每层院落另砌围墙和门楼,门楼上的门楣用木头刻有"树德物滋"字样至今保存完好。

A century-old cave Dwelling

With all stone masonry by exquisite craft, the old cave was built along the hill. And the stone-step path is still solid after a hundred years. The cave is divided into three layers: Upper, middle and lower layer. The upper layer is still occupied by people. The middle layer remains intact, but is no longer inhabited. The lower one is used for livestock breeding and storage, and now lays idle.

黄土窑洞

  黄土地上的窑洞是与地形气候密切相关的独特民居形式,时至今日窑洞依然有它存在的优势与理由,不但与黄土高原形成特有的风景,而且形成了特有的窑洞文化。

Loess Cave Dwelling

The cave dwelling is a unique residential building closely related to climate and terrain. Today, the cave still has advantages and reasons for its existence. Cave dwelling not only forms unique scenery with the Loess Plateau, but also forms special cave dwelling culture.

窑洞旁的枣林（一）

村子里每家的房前房后都有许多枣树，不少人还在山上种植了大片的枣树，上山的小路上到处都落有枣，老乡的院子里晒着一片一片的枣。

Jujube Forest Near Cave Dwellings (1)

In the village, there are many jujube trees in front of each house. Quite a few people grow large jujube trees on the mountain. Along the path up the hill, jujube trees are everywhere. Villager yards are covered with jujubes drying in the sun.

窑洞旁的枣林（二）

　　枣树种在山坡上下，窑洞筑在山坡中间，间有小道四通八达。一到夏天满山一片绿色，透过绿荫，时有窑洞显露其间。到了秋天，满树红枣挂满枝头，点点红色，点缀在黄土高坡上。

Jujube Forest Near Cave Dwellings (2)

Jujube trees are planted up and down the hillside, and caves are built in the middle of the hillside, with paths extending in all directions. In summer, the hill is covered with green, and the cave is revealed through the shade showing its white walls, unpainted wooden doors and windows. In autumn, the tree branches are full of red jujubes, like little red dots in the Loess plateau.

窑洞旁的枣林（三）

　　这一带的枣树，有的树龄已达数百年，与最早的窑洞属同一年代。如今仍然青翠，枝叶繁盛，树干粗近碗口，窑洞与枣树相映成趣。枣树的枝干有硬度而富有弹性，窑洞的石痕斑驳又显得沧桑，窑洞前没有枣树显不出完美，枣树间缺少窑洞也显得缺少韵律。

Jujube Forest Near Cave Dwellings (3)
Some of the jujube trees in this area are hundreds of years old, dating back to the ages of the earliest cave dwelling. These trees are still verdant, with vigorous foliage, branch in coarse sized, cave and jujube trees forming delightful contrast. Jujube branches feature hardness and elastic, while mottled marks on cave stone reveal vicissitudes. Without jujube trees, the cave would not be perfect, and without the cave, jujube trees would appear monotonous.

窑洞旁的枣林（四）

在层层窑洞之间你能看到这样的景色。春天一抹浅绿，为黄土高坡带来生机；夏季的深绿又让人感到这里还是比较温润的；秋季的这里黄色丰富，更显出一份富贵之色；到了冬天遇有霜挂满树，那黄土高原显得圣洁优美。

Jujube Forest Near Cave Dwellings (4)

You can see such views among the caves. In spring, light green brings vitality to the Loess plateau. In summer, deep green makes people feel quite warm and humid. In autumn, the rich yellow showcases the abundance. In winter, trees covered with frost making the Loess Plateau look holy and graceful.

窑门（一）

　　米脂窑洞多为木门，尤其是旧窑洞，门窗多有雕花四方连续图案，设计美观大方式样丰富。窗棂多在屋里糊有窗纸，为防止雨水打湿曾有用桐油将糊好的窗纸（以前用的窗纸多为手工制造的麻纸）涂抹。

The Gate of Cave (1)

Most caves in Mizhi County, especially the old ones, have wooden doors. The doors and windows are carved in square patterns, elegant and various. Most window frames are pasted with paper, and to prevent rainwater, the paper is painted with tung oil (previous paper is handmade hemp paper).

窑门（二）

　　这些木门窗，有的窗棂可部分翻转，以便于通风。也有的将纸制成卷帘，用线绷在窗户上，通风时卷起，放下时防尘，不过现在已少用此法了。随着钢门窗和铝合金门窗的使用，木质门窗已渐渐退出家庭装修的舞台。

The Gate of Cave (2)

As for these wooden doors and windows, some windows can be partially turned for ventilation, and some windows are covered with rolling paper as curtain, tied on the window, rolled up to ventilate and rolled down to prevent dust from entering. But now this method is outdated. With the use of steel or aluminum alloy windows, wooden doors and windows have gradually been obsolete in family decoration.

窑门（三）

现在许多新窑洞除了使用材料更新外，式样、装修效果也比以前讲究了。门框、洞门、窗户都更讲究整齐、实用、美观、大方，体现出现代美观和新的精神面貌。这样的窑洞除了外观上的变化之外，家用电器也跟城市一样。窑洞居民的生活质量和面貌发生着巨大的改变。

The Gate of Cave (3)

Now, for many new caves, style and decoration are more exquisite than before, in addition to updated materials. The door and windows are more neat, functional, beautiful and dignified, embodying modern aesthetics and new spirit. Except changes in appearance, caves have the same household appliances as in city.

窑门（四）

一个窑洞经过百年的洗礼，渐渐磨掉新建时石头的菱角，保留下的是朴素的本质，雕琢的痕迹渐渐淡化，显现的是石与石之间经过风霜雪雨洗礼更自然的吻合。百年沧桑更迭的是窑洞的主人，延续的是美丽。

The Gate of Cave (4)

After hundreds of years weathering, the corners of stone have gradually been worn down, only plain nature preserved. Carved marks gradually fade, and the closeness of stones becomes more tight after weathering. During the hundred-year vicissitudes, the owners of the cave have been changing, but the beauty of the cave remains.

窑门（五）

一排改作储草的老窑洞，被阴影遮挡只露出一片斑驳的石墙面，近处几枝枣树穿插期间，窑洞在余晖的光照下所产生的大小不一的光斑，给人以岁月沧桑的感觉。岁月不断成为往事，但闪光将永远保持在记忆中。

The Gate of Cave (5)

A row of old caves is used as storehouse for grass. Shade only reveals a mottled stone wall, with several Jujube branches touched. The sunlight spots on the cave make people think about its history. Time always passes by, but the image always remains in memory.

窑门（六）

　　这是一个破旧的窑洞，四周的泥土已开始塌落，虽然仅存半截窗棂，但依稀能看出当年的精美，这一切将随着时间慢慢消失。在窑洞前有一个玉米垛，给人感觉新生命能量的聚集。

The Gate of Cave (6)

This is a worn-out cave, around which the soil has begun to collapse, but from the only half of the window lattice, you can almost see the exquisite craft at that time. However, all this will fade away with time. There is a corn pile in front of the cave, making people sense the accumulation of new life energy.

窑门（七）

在黄土高坡上有很多这样的窑洞，挖在半地下的，口不很大，但里面很深很大，主要是用来储存过冬农副产品，如土豆、白菜，还有苹果、梨等。里面的温度很低，储存的东西能保鲜，有的可以放到来年的盛夏。

The Gate of Cave (7)

There are so many such caves in the Loess Plateau, dug in the semi underground, with a small entrance. But inside, it is deep and large, mainly used for winter storage of agricultural and sideline products. Potatoes and cabbage, apple, pear, can be stored until the next summer. The temperature in cave is very low, so it can keep things fresh.

窑门（八）

　　这是个很别致的窑洞门，窑门尖尖的，听当地的老人讲这种窑大多都是外乡人来这里建的，都是较小的窑洞，现在已经不建了，留下来的已经非常少。

The Gate of Cave (8)

This is a very unique gate of a cave, with a sharp top. Local people say this kind is mostly built by non-native people, and very few are now built.

门楼（一）

门楼是窑洞建筑相配套的重要组成部分。这里有相当多的门楼是用石头建的，门楼的两侧墙都是方正的石头砌成，虽然石头有大小，但角和面都很整齐，门楼的房沿和瓦片全是选用片石砌成（这里山沟下面有种石片可采）。门框、门楣、檩子、橡子都是采自当地硬杂木。这是门楼经年坚固不毁的重要原因之一，看上去也非常的朴素大方。

Gatehouse (1)

The gatehouse is an important part of the cave building. Quite a lot of the gatehouses are built of stone, and both side walls are built with square stones. Although the stones are small, but the angle and the surface is clean and tidy. Tiles on the gatehouse roof are cleft stones (below a ravine, cleft stones can be mined).

门楼（二）

这是一处在坡上修建的门楼，碾子放在院外比较宽敞的地方，门前还有棵枣树给窑洞一片荫凉。整个小景好像是有意安排的，但在这荒芜的高坡上谁又会这么做呢？这也许就是生活中的美吧。

Gatehouse (2)

This gatehouse is built on a slope, and the stone roller is placed in the spacious yard. In front of the door, a jujube tree casts a shade for the cave. The whole scene seems to be intentional, but on this desolate hillside, who could do that? Maybe this is exactly the beauty of life.

门楼（三）

利用门楼的题字传播中华文明的优良品德是村里人的通常作法，要知道这在几百年前的偏僻小村，以务农为主，又不富裕的乡民来说，花费这么大的功夫，可见那时人们对中国传统文化的崇拜和信仰。

Gatehouse (3)

Gate inscription is normally used by villagers to spread Chinese ethics. A few hundred years ago, in this remote village, the people who are mainly farmers and not rich, made so much effort to show their worship and belief in Chinese traditional culture.

门楼（四）

　　黄土高原上窑洞建筑使用了大量的石材。石头的围墙，石头的小屋，石头的门楼，石头铺的山路，石头碾子，石头磨盘，石头的草料槽和水槽。就连窑洞房沿瓦片也是用石头的天然形状砌筑而成，说是石头的世界一点也不过份。

Gatehouse (4)

Many cave buildings on the Loess Plateau are built with a lot of stones. Walls, huts, gatehouses, roads, rollers, mills, hayracks and sinks, are all made with stones, and even the roof tiles are also raw stones, totally a stone fairyland.

门楼（五）

中国的北方院落，多有院门，无论朝西、朝东、朝南，少不了向阳的时候。只要在阳光下，就能折射出生活的气息。早晨能使人出门见到阳光，精神每一天，晚上回家，仍能看到落日的余辉。

Gatehouse (5)

In North China, a courtyard, towards whichever direction, can get sunlight in the daytime. As long as in the sun, you can sense the breath of life. In the morning, sunshine can make people feel fresh for a whole day, while at dusk, people still can see the afterglow of the setting sun when coming back home.

门楼（六）

　　在这里，老门楼就是传承的象征。一个老院，一个门楼，一用就是数百年，几代人进进出出，从没有嫌弃老祖宗留下宝贵遗产。历经百年虽能看到修补的痕迹，但修的仔细，补的整齐，一点没有影响门的质量和美观。

Gatehouse (6)

Here, the old gatehouse is a kind of heritage. An old courtyard, or a gatehouse, can be used for hundreds of years. Generation after generation, these precious legacies have never been abandoned. After a hundred year, although we can see the signs of mending, but the careful and neat repair does not affect the quality and beauty of the door.

门楼（七）

傍晚前的阳光渐渐变成金色，这山峦、树林、窑洞，连围墙也不例外的笼罩在灿烂的阳光里。由于光线强烈，这整个山村像是一幅套色木刻，鲜明的明暗对比，突出了阳光给人带来温暖感觉，晚霞映出石墙的斑驳增加了不少凝重感。似剪影式的人物慢慢走在山路上，像是品味这浓厚的生活。

Gatehouse (7)

The evening sun turns golden, and the hills, woods, and caves, including the wall, are enveloped in brilliant sunshine. Because the light is strong, the whole village is like a colored woodcut, bright contrast, highlighting the sun bringing warm feeling to people, and the mottled stone reflected by sunset increases a somewhat dignified sense. Silhouette like, a person slowly reaches the distance, as if it is tasting this strong coffee of life.

门楼（八）

老门楼旁矗立着一棵300多年的老树，夹杂着夕阳，给人一种宁静的田园心境。

Gatehouse (8)

Next to the old gatehouse stands an old tree of more than 300 years, along with the setting sun, making a peaceful pastoral scenery.

夯土墙

这种墙是用土夯出来的墙，由于长期间风雨侵蚀变得轮廓模糊。图是黄土坡土窑洞冬天雪后的景色。

Loam Wall

This kind of wall is rammed out of earth, and its contour becomes blurred due to long periods of wind and rain. The above sketch depicts winter scenery of the Loess Slope caves after snow.

巷 道

在一个不宽的山沟两侧分别建有石砌窑洞,相对的窑洞中间有一条通往山上的小道。这小道是山上山下乡民过往的必经之路。巷道两侧围墙虽属各家,但整个巷道基本整齐砌筑成一条线也是窑洞民居一处有特点的景观。

Laneway

On both sides of a narrow valley stands stone caves. A laneway goes up the hill between the opposing caves, and it is the only way for the villagers to go up and down. For convenience of living and passing through, between the caves on both sides is three-meters-wide laneway. Although each sidewall belongs to different households, the masonry neatly almost in a line is also a characteristic landscape of cave dwellings.

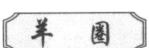

这个羊圈是由窑洞和外面的石砌圈结合起来的,也属黄土高原特有。在羊圈边上还栽着一些枣树。这幅画面来源于生活的真实,但却显得新鲜,自然和构图上的完美。画面中黑白灰构成、对比协调,动与静都有体现。

Sheepfold

This Sheepfold is formed by the outside of the cave and stone circle, which is also unique for the Loess Plateau. There are some jujube trees on the edge of the sheepfold. This picture comes from the true portrayal of life, but it looks fresh, natural and perfect. In the picture, layout of black, white and grey, contrast and coordination, movement and stillness, all these are depicted.

柴草堆（一）

这里至今仍保留着用牛耕作的方式。放草料的地方几乎家家都有，也算是目前耕作的一个特征。从现象上看有些原始，但从造型上看，这场面也是珍贵的，用不了几年，这里的面貌将彻底改变。

Firewood (1)

Farming with cattle is still in use here. Almost every family has a place for fodder, which is also a characteristic of current farming. It appears to be primitive, but, in terms of its shape, the scene is precious. Because in a few years, it will change completely.

柴草堆（二）

在院子边和坡上堆满了柴草。这柴的用途也是很多的，秸秆用来喂牛，树枝与茬根用来烧饭。还有一些檩条和旁边堆砌的石料，那是准备盖新窑洞用的。

Firewood (2)

On the edge of the yard and the slope, firewood is piled everywhere, and its usages are versatile. Straw is used to feed the cattle, while branches and stubble are used for cooking. Some piled purlins and stones stacked, are prepared to build a new cave.

碾子（一）

这是一个较大的院子，夕阳下一片安静，碾子在院子里分外显眼，反映着这里人们的生活方式和生产水平。尽管这里通了公路，增加了与外界的联系，但传统的老式生活节奏并没有根本改变，这样的场景很象是历史的定格。

Stone Roller (1)

This is a large courtyard, quiet in the sunset, and a pair of stone rollers are conspicuous in the yard, showing local people's life style and production level. Although the road has improved the connection with the outside world, the traditional rhythm of the old life has not been changed fundamentally, and such a scene is just like a freeze frame of history.

碾子（二）

一只巨大的碾子停在碾盘上，由于长期使用，碾盘被磨得铮亮，碾盘现出深深的裂痕，说明它曾经的力量。如今时代进步的速度令人无法想象，使用碾子的场景已经退出了人们生活的视线。

Stone Roller (2)

A huge roller is on the grinding base, which has been polished and shows deep fissures due to the long-term use. The huge stone roller indicates its previous power and merits. Now the progress of the times is unimaginable, the scene of using stone roller will gradually disappear.

黄土风情
Customs of the Loess Plateau

耕地（一）

耕地在农村是非常重要的农活，一是要遵从时令，有"人误地一时，地误人一年"之说；二是劳动强度大；三是劳动时间长，从村里走到要耕的地里要走几里路或更远的山坡才能到达，要计算花在路上需要的时间，有时为了节省时间早晨天不亮就开始往地里走，无论耕到什么时间，不耕完不回来。这一天的劳动是以完成任务为目标，不是像城里人按规律时间定作息，地块小也可能上午10点就完成任务了，也许一去就要连续干一天到晚上才回来。

Ploughing (1)

Ploughing is very important in villages. First, ploughing must fit in season, "Once you missed the timing of ploughing, the farmland would be wasted for a year". Second, ploughing is highly intensive labor. Third, the time spent on ploughing is very long, because the journey from village to farmland may be a few miles, sometimes even mountain road, which is time consuming. To save time, the journey begins before dawn, and no matter how long the plowing lasts, only when it is finished will farmers go back home.

耕地（二）

在高高的山坡上，两个人赶着一头牛正在播种。阳光照在他们身上显出明亮的结构，整块的大地显示出土地的厚重与博大，他们不仅播种的是粮食种子，也播种着幸福和希望。

Ploughing (2)

On the farmland along hillside, two men are sowing with a farm cattle. The sunlight on them forms a bright silhouette, and the boundless ground shows its grandness. What they are sowing are seeds of crop, happiness and hope.

耕地（三）

耕牛耕平地很自然，耕山坡地还是少见。这里有相当多的土地是坡地，用牛耕坡地作为当地人已习以为常，但没有经验是做不到的。

Ploughing (3)

It is natural to see farm cattle for flat ground, but rare for slope ground. Local people have become accustomed to cultivating slopes with cattle, but it is impossible if without experience.

耕地（四）

这里许多地都在山上，没有梯田的平整，而是倾斜的山坡地，小型手扶拖拉机在耕作时还要一个人用绳子拉住保持平衡，否则会掉下去，像杂技表演。试想在斜度超过三十度的山坡上耕作或收获是多么不容易的事情，真是那句话，"谁知盘中餐，粒粒皆辛苦"。

Ploughing (4)
Much of cultivated land is on the hill, without the formation like terraced fields, only sloping hillside. When cultivating, the small tractor must be dragged with a rope to keep it balance, otherwise it will fall off, like an acrobatic show.

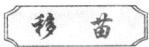

   在沿河的滩地上，土地湿润，适宜种菜。当地人往往不失时节地移栽菜苗，而从事这些农活的除了当地老年人就是妇女，还有一些未成年的孩子。能直接参与和了解农业生产，不仅是未成年人的重要学习机会，更重要的是从小培养了对劳动的认识和态度。

Transplanting

On the beach along the river, the land is wet and suitable for growing vegetables. Local residents often transplant vegetable seedlings in proper season. And those who do farm work, are the elder or women, as well as some underage children. Being able to directly participate in and understand agricultural production is an important learning opportunity for minors, and more significantly, it cultivates their knowledge and attitude toward labor from an early age.

捡土豆

秋天收获的土豆要分类筛选，根据质量和用途分别出吃食用的、做种子的和销售的。由于当地青壮劳力大量外出打工，这个细心、耗时，看似简单实则费力的工作只能落到带着孩子的妇女和老人身上。

Picking potatoes

Harvested potatoes should be classified separately in autumn, according to quality and purpose for food, seed or sale. Because a large number of the young labor force have emigrated to the city for work, the seemingly simple but time-consuming work falls on women with children and elderly people.

> 收秋菜

　　在农作物收获完之后，就开始收获小面积的蔬菜，这些蔬菜是在大宗作物的地边或较湿润的地方种植的。这些秋菜或便于冬储，如土豆、白菜、萝卜；或便于腌制，如白菜、芹菜、香菜等，因品种不同，收获也要分类进行。

Collecting Autumn Vegetable
After the crops are harvested, they begin harvesting small areas of vegetables, which are grown on the edge of the crop or the wetter areas. Some autumn vegetables are suitable for the winter storage, such as potatoes, cabbage, radish; some are easy to be pickled, such as cabbage, celery, coriander. Different categories are processed differently.

碾"钱钱儿"

　　碾"钱钱儿"是晋陕一带用黄豆压成片状食品的加工方法。"钱钱儿"可用来煮粥。口感好，易消化，熟得快。当地虽有电磨或电碾子加工，但老年人仍然喜欢用石碾子加工"钱钱儿"。

Grinding Qianqian

Grinding Qianqian is the processing method by which soybeans are pressed into flake food in Shanxi and shaanxi. Qianqian tastes good, easy to digest and convenient to cook. Although the processing mill and electric roller are available, older people still use stone roller to process Qianqian.

碾豆子

　　碾豆子的是一对老夫妻。他们也是这里的老住户,儿女外出打工,他们不愿住在城市里,住惯了这里的窑洞,听惯了这里的鸟叫,这里没有城市的喧闹,但也衣食无忧。

Grinding beans

An old couple are grinding beans. They are long-time residents here. Their children have emigrated to the city for work, but they do not want to live in the city, because they are used to living here, listening to birds, without noise or worrying about food and clothing.

背柴

　　这里的村民生活燃料主要是柴，各家所属地块的果木更新及农作物秸杆都可做为柴供烧火用。因为这里枣树多，每年也要剪枝，如不剪枝枣就结的很少，所以这里的人们大量用枣树枝作为柴火。

Carring Firewood

The villagers mainly use firewood for living. Outdated fruit branches and harvested crop straw can be used as firewood. Because a large numbers of jujube trees are pruned every year, for yielding more jujubes, so local people use plenty of jujube branches as firewood.

| 劈 柴 |

　　除了能剪下来的枣树枝叉可以当柴以外，这里的死树根和一些成不了材的树干同样可作柴烧，但必须伐倒、自然风干，为了节省占地也有要锯成一定长度后码放整齐以备用。风干后的木段，再劈成可烧的柴。

Chopping Firewood

In addition to outdated jujube branches that can be used as firewood, the dead tree roots and some tree trunks that can't be made into timber can also be used for firewood. But they must be cut down for drying naturally, and then be sawed into short pieces in order to be put aside neatly, saving storage space.

拉草料（一）

村里喂牛的草料，多为禾本科农作物的秸杆。在穗头收完以后，剩下的都作为饲料，可以择时将其陆续拉回来。因秸杆分散在不同方向，不同高度的分散地块，用车拉也是一件辛苦的事情。因为是山路转弯、上坡、保持车的平衡并需要足够的体力。现在年轻人都进城了，这样的活，主要是上了年纪的老年人干。

Carrying fodder (1)

The fodder for cattle feeding in villages are mostly straw of gramineous crops. After the ear of rice has been harvested, the rest will be used as fodder, and pulled back home bit by bit. Because straw is from farm in different directions and heights, so its carrying by cart is also a hard work.

拉草料（二）

赶着牛车拉草料，一路走一路哼着山曲，把劳动当成一种快乐。这里有许多老人，子女已在城里定居，他们却不愿随儿女进城。他们现在还有政府发的老年补贴，自己再做点农活，生活没有问题。他们喜欢这里的一山一水，每天闲不住总有自己想干的农活。

Carrying fodder (2)

Driving the ox cart with fodder, walking and singing all the way, gives people the joy of labor. Many old people whose children have settled down in the city, are not willing to go into town with their children. They love local hills and streams, and every day they are restless from farm work they want to do.

铡 草

　　这户人家养着一头牛，前两天老牛生下一只小牛，一家人很高兴准备过几年小牛长大，就能卖个好价钱。这两位老人已年过六旬，强体力劳动已不适应他们，他们只能做些身体能适应的较轻一点的事，养牛是一项不错的选择。

Chopping Fodder

This household raises a cow. Two days ago, the cow gave birth to a calf, which made the family very pleased. They prepare to sell the calf at a good price when it grows up a few years later. The old couple are over sixty, so they cannot adapt to toilsome labor. They want to do some easy work, such as raising cattle.

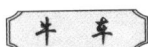

　　这里的牛除了耕地外还用来驾车拉运上山下山的物资，如农具、粮食、草料等。牛也有劲，是农民的好帮手。山区小片地分散，增加路途时间的耗费，许多年纪大的农民不适应使用农用拖拉机，不仅会增加耗费的油钱，还要掌握临时故障的处理和日常维护，而牛仅需要喂草料就行了。

Ox Cart
Except for ploughing, oxen are also used to carry a cart with materials up and down the hill, such as farm tools, grain, forage and so on. The oxen are strong, and good helpers to the farmers. The farm on the hill is scattered, needing more time for the journey. Many older farmers are not accustomed to farm tractors, while the ox is familiar with the hill road, so the journey is more safe.

锯木头

这是一户农民翻新自家窑洞的场景。将院内一颗大树伐倒以拓宽用地。这里窑洞居多，当地伐倒的大树也没有买来的建材好用，所以这些木材一般不作为建筑材料使用。

Sawing Wood

This is the scene where a family are renovating their own cave, they are cutting down a big tree in the courtyard to make room for the foundation. Most houses are caves, and felled trees are not as useful as bought materials, so generally these trunks are not used as building materials.

打 铁

　　铁匠铺在城里已看不到，而这里农村仍保留着非机械化耕种习惯，老式手工农具仍在使用，就有了铁匠铺存在空间。谁家的锄头坏了，农具中某个铁质部件修复非得用传统铁匠手艺修复不可。

Blacksmithing

The blacksmith shop in the city no longer exist, but in villages where the non-mechanized farming still uses traditional farming tools. Therefore, the blacksmith shop has a use. When someone's hoes or iron parts of farm tools are broken, the restoration must be done by traditional blacksmith.

看戏

　　看戏是村里组织的大型活动,喜欢观看的多数是老年人。剧团人员在村中的戏台上演出,观众在台下露天空地上看。老年人搬上自己的小板凳选择较好位置坐下,而年青人没有吵闹的,也没有和老年人抢地方的。他们只是静静地站在后面或坐在后面,整个看戏秩序井然。即便是有些卖小吃、杂物的也没有高声叫卖的,并离看戏地有很大距离,不影响看戏。看的人全神贯注,演的人认真卖力。

Watching Plays
Watching Plays is a major activity in villages and most of the audience are elderly people. The actors perform at the village stage, and the audience watch in the open air. Older people carrying campstools choose a better place to sit down, while young people sit or stand behind them quietly with no quarrel. The audience are absorbed, and the performers are devoted.

社 火

　　每年农历三月十八日，村里都要举办大型社火，一般举办三天。附近乡村都有人来，一早上就有三五成群的民众陆续赶来，有的坐着农用车来的，有骑摩托车来的，还有祭祀的队伍举着祭祀的旗帜。抬着山神的神位在乐手吹打声中缓缓走来，在村内广场上扭起秧歌。

Shehuo Carnival

On lunar March 18th, annual Shehuo Carnival is held in the village, usually lasting for three days. People from the nearby villages also come to this gathering. Early in the morning, some people arrive, riding by agricultural vehicles or motorcycles, and some people carrying the sacrifice flag and a spirit tablet of the Mountain God, walking slowly with the percussion sound by musicians, and begin to perform Yangko dance once reaching the village square.

吃过晚饭，人们习惯三五成群坐在树下、路边聊天。这里民歌很好听，有时晚上周围村民无事便高歌一曲，有好事的就接着对唱起来。这里村民朴实纯真，他们歌唱没有拿捏造作，没有修饰。

Singing together

After supper, villagers are used to sitting together under trees or by the roadside to chat. Folk songs here are very pleasant. Sometimes villagers sing a song for fun, and then someone interested will sing to it. Villagers here have a rich regional culture, and their songs are innocent and natural.

村 妇

这里的人热情好客而且朴实真诚。我们走在村子里,当地老乡全主动与你打招呼:"你们是从哪里来的,进屋里坐坐,喝点水,吃苹果。"住户的厨房,干净简朴,看来平日也是这样,给我的感觉是真诚、朴实。

Village Woman

Residents here are hospitable and honest. When we were walking in the village, and all of the local villagers greet you warmly." Where do you come from? Come in and take a seat. drink some water and eat some apples." The village kitchen is clean and simple, it seems so every day. All this shows their sincerity and simplicity.

婆姨

"米脂的婆姨，绥德的汉"这句话很多人都听到过。"婆姨"在陕北是指结了婚的妇女。来到米脂后才知道这句话的真正意义。因为他们孝老爱亲，勤劳善良，善于持家，保持和继承了中华民族的传统美德而被处处传颂。

Poyi aunt

As is known to many people, "Poyi aunts from MiZhi County are good, and so are uncles from SuiDe County". "Poyi aunt" refers to married women in Northern Shaanxi. The true meaning of this sentence can be truly understood when you come to MiZhi County. Because of their filial piety, diligence, kindness, and good housekeeping, all these Chinese traditional virtues of the nation are praised by people everywhere.

孩子（一）

与城里孩子上学截然不同，这里的孩子都是自己背着书包上学的，自己走着去，自己走着回来，自己拿钥匙开门。甚至夜间村里有电影或演戏，他们有住在学校的学生自己去看，没有大人的陪护。放学以后，他们没有城里孩子那样有自己的桌子、房间和家长的叮嘱。他们自己找块平坦的碾盘、石桌或一块较平的石板当做"桌子"，就趴在上面写作业。他们不仅是学习，还要帮助家中做家务，或参加农业生产。他们的自理能力明显要比城市孩子强。

Children (1)

Quite different from kids in the city, children here are seen carrying schoolbags to school by themselves. They Walk to and back from school, and take the key to open the door also by themselves. Students who live in school even go to see movies or plays in the village during the evening alone, without the accompany of adults.

孩子（二）

农村的孩子没有城市孩子那么多的玩具和活动场所。他们经常在自己家附近的山坡上下，或随意拿些简单的东西做玩具或一根树枝或路边采一朵野花。我曾问过一个快要上中学的孩子是否愿意去城里上学。他们的回答让我感到意外，他说："我爸妈都在西安生活，我喜欢乡下清新的空气和安静的生活。这里有我的爷爷奶奶，我喜欢和他们在一起。不喜欢西安那样的大城市，太嘈杂。"

Children (2)

Children in rural areas do not have as many toys or activities as city children. They often go up and down the hillside near their home or pick up something simple as a toy, maybe a piece of branch, or a wild flower by the road. I once asked a child who was nearly at high school age if he wanted to go to school in the city. His answer surprised me. He said, "My parents are living in Xi'an, but I love the fresh air and quiet life in the village. Our grandparents are still here, I like to be with them. I don't like big cities like Xi'an, too noisy and too many cars."

孩子（三）

　　中华民族自古以来就有尊老爱幼的美德。爱幼也是与尊老互为转化，互相依存的，从小培养儿童的爱心，也是言传身教的。这不仅是理论上的说教，更重要的是身教，有爱心才能友善。尊老爱幼是传统美德，就需要不断地传承，不断地践行。

Children (3)

The Chinese nation has the ancient virtue to respect the elder and love the young. Loving the young and respecting the elder bring out the best in each other. Children's love need to be cultivated by precept and example from childhood. This traditional virtue needs to be continuously carried on and practiced.

　　串门聊天是这里的一种生活常态。他们不仅在闲时聊天，就连吃饭时也喜欢揣着碗饭去串门，一边吃饭，一边聊天，吃完了回去盛上饭菜再过来。吃饭也是他们交流信息，互通信息的手段。在自己家窑洞前聊天是很常见的。

Dropping in

Dropping in a friend's home to chat is common here. They chat not only in leisure time. Some people even drop in with hands holding their bowls while having a meal, and as soon as the bowl is empty, they go back home to fill it and come back again. Chatting over a meal is also a means of learning about things.